God Made Us, And He Does Not Make Junk

Stronger Together

Cindy H. Carr, D.Min., MACL

This book is published by **CHC Connect**.

Printed in the United States of America
First Edition, 2025

ISBN: 978-1-971192-05-5

For permissions or inquiries, contact:
Cindy H. Carr
cindyhcarr@outlook.com
www.cindyhcarr.com

About This Series

In a world that often questions our worth, **The Made by God Series** gently brings us back to a simple, powerful truth: God created each of us with intention, care, and purpose.

This series leads readers on a journey—from understanding who you are in God's eyes, to recognizing His unique design in others, to living together in authentic, life-giving community. With warmth and clarity you see that every person bears God's imprint, and that we are meant to live that truth out together.

Because God made you, God made them, and together, God made us—and He does not make junk.

- **Book 1**
  God Made You, And He Does Not Make Junk: Discovering the You That God Had in Mind
- **Book 2**
  God Made Them, And He Does Not Make Junk: Honoring God's Creativity in Others
- **Book 3**
  God Made Us, And He Does Not Make Junk: Stronger Together

Visit www.cindyhcarr.com to view the full catalog.

Acknowledgments

I want to begin by acknowledging my family because *God Made Us, And He Doesn't Make Junk* is about learning to live as "us," and family is where that lesson becomes real. Other types of communities often give us space to come in and go out, but family is the place you live with people up close—day after day, 24/7. It's where character is built the strongest, where love is tested and practiced, and where what we believe has to become how we live. From there, we learn how to carry that same kind of honor, respect, and connection into every other community we're a part of.

Introduction

If you've walked with me through Book 1, God Made You and He Does Not Make Junk, you know the moment I love most—the lights come on and you realize, "Oh… this is how God designed me." There's a calm confidence when you stop copying others and start living as the person God actually made.

Then Book 2, God Made Them and He Does Not Make Junk, expanded the joy. Once you start seeing God's creativity in others, you notice how He "thinks in variety"—different strengths, rhythms, temperaments—and recognize that those differences often carry gifts you don't personally have.

Now comes Book 3: how do we build a life together that actually works? This one's about the "us"—real marriages, families, teams, neighborhoods, and communities where people learn how to belong, contribute, and grow without losing themselves.

Healthy community doesn't happen by accident. It's built—through choices like honor, curiosity, clear communication, quick repair, and clean boundaries. Scripture will stay close, not as a test but as a steady light.

I'm writing with you, not at you—as if we're sharing coffee, laughter, and truth. My prayer is simple: that you'll feel hopeful and equipped, ready to build "us"—a community that reflects heaven more than survival.

Table of Contents

How to Use This Book

This book is written like a coaching conversation—practical, warm, and meant to be lived, not just admired.

Read straight through—or jump to what you need

You can read from Chapter 1 to the end and follow the build: foundation → practices → real-life places → a simple blueprint. Or you can jump to the area you need most right now: marriage, parenting, friendships, workplace culture, conflict, boundaries, or leadership.

Practice one small thing at a time

Most chapters include a "Try this sentence." That's on purpose. You don't need more theory—you need words you can use in the kitchen, in the meeting, or in the car on the way home. Pick one sentence and try it once this week. That's enough. (No heavy homework. We're building real life, not a binder.)

Use reflection as optional

Each chapter includes a short reflection. If you love journaling, it's for you. If journaling makes you feel itchy, you have full permission to skip it. Some people process by writing. Others process by walking, praying, or talking it out. God is not grading you.

Remember the goal: culture, not chemistry

Chemistry is "we click." Culture is "we can thrive even when we don't click." This book helps you build culture: shared values, shared purpose, shared respect—and the skills that keep relationships healthy when opinions differ.

A simple rhythm (if you want one)

1) Read one chapter.
2) Choose one "Try this sentence."
3) Use it once this week.
4) If you mess it up, repair quickly. (That counts as progress.)

Chapter 1: Not Alone on Purpose — Connection Was God's Design

If you want to understand the "us," you have to start where God started: relationship.

Before there were families, workplaces, friendships, or communities, there was God—Father, Son, and Holy Spirit. God is not lonely. God is love. And love, by its nature, is relational.

So when Scripture says we are made in His image, it's not just talking about individual dignity (though it absolutely includes that). It's also pointing to something communal: we are designed for connection. Not shallow connection—real connection. The kind that forms you. The kind that stretches you. The kind that teaches you love.

The first "not good" in the Bible

Genesis is full of "good." God creates, and He calls it good. Again and again. But then something surprising shows up: "It is not good for the man to be alone" (Genesis 2:18, NIV).

Notice what's happening. Adam is in a perfect environment. He has purpose. He has access to God. And still—alone is not the goal.

That line doesn't mean everyone has to be married to be whole. It means isolation was never God's design. You were not created to carry your whole life by yourself—your joys, your burdens, your questions, your callings, your griefs.

And if you've ever thought, "I love God, but people are exhausting," you are not disqualified from this message. You're just honest.

The goal of community isn't constant togetherness. The goal is meaningful connection—the kind that strengthens you and strengthens others.

Why community feels hard

Here's why the "us" can feel complicated: community brings us face-to-face with difference.

If you're building a life with real humans, you're going to meet different rhythms, different priorities, different communication styles, different emotional ranges, different ways of processing stress.

Sometimes we interpret difference as threat. Sometimes we interpret it as rejection. Sometimes we interpret it as disrespect.

But what if difference isn't danger? What if it's design?

If Book 2 taught us to recognize God's creativity in others, Book 3 helps us build something with it—a way of doing "us" that doesn't require sameness.

The Bible calls it "one another"

One of my favorite things about Scripture is how practical it is. The New Testament is filled with "one another" language:

Love one another. Encourage one another. Forgive one another. Bear with one another. Carry each other's burdens. Build each other up.

That's not abstract spirituality. That's a community blueprint.

And here's the quiet miracle: you can't practice "one another" alone. Which means community isn't a side quest. It's part of spiritual formation.

A quick picture: the body needs more than one part

Paul says it plainly: we are "one body," with "many parts" (Romans 12:4–5, NIV). Different parts, one purpose.

So if you've ever felt like you don't belong because you're different, hear me: difference isn't a disqualifier—it's evidence you're needed.

A healthy "us" doesn't require everyone to be the same. It requires everyone to be honored—and aligned around the main thing.

The main thing we're building

This book is going to keep returning to one simple foundation: families are built on more than preferences, friendships are built on more than matching opinions, and teams are built on more than identical personalities. They're built on shared values, shared purpose, and shared respect.

When those three are present, people can disagree and still stay connected. When those three are absent, even people who "match" can become toxic.

And if you're thinking, "Okay, but how do we actually build that?"—good. That's where we're going.

Try this sentence

"I want us to build something healthy together—can we name what matters most to both of us?"

Optional reflection

1) Where do you feel the most 'us' right now—home, friendships, work, or community?

2) Where do you feel the least 'us'—and what do you think is missing (values, purpose, respect, or skills)?

3) What would "healthy us" look like in one sentence?

Prayer

Father, thank You that You created us for connection. Teach me to build with honor, not fear. Give me wisdom to create shared values, shared purpose, and shared respect wherever You've placed me. Help me practice love in real time—patient, kind, truthful, and strong. In Jesus' name, amen.

Bridge to Chapter 2

In Chapter 2, we'll talk about unity without sameness—how to stay connected when you don't agree, and how to keep the main thing the main thing.

Chapter 2: Unity Without Sameness — When Agreement Isn't Required

One of the greatest lies we can believe about relationships is this: if we love each other, we'll see everything the same.

That sounds sweet… until you share a home, raise kids, lead a team, or try to plan a vacation with people who pack like they're moving.

Real life quickly reveals the truth: love doesn't erase difference. Love learns to carry it.

Years ago, God gave me a simple revelation that has shaped how I relate to people: unity is not always agreement.

Unity means we stay connected around what matters most. Agreement means we share the same opinion, preference, or method.

You can have unity without agreement. And you can have agreement without unity—just ask anyone who has ever "agreed" on the outside while quietly resenting each other on the inside.

Unity is a covenant; agreement is a condition

Agreement tends to be conditional: "If you see it my way, we're good."

Unity is relational: "Even if we don't see it the same way, we're going to stay in honor, stay truthful, and keep moving toward the main thing."

Unity doesn't mean you avoid hard conversations. It means you refuse to use difference as an excuse to dishonor each other.

Think about how Jesus built His team. He didn't pick twelve men with matching temperaments and identical perspectives.

He chose different personalities, different backgrounds, and different ways of processing—then He taught them how to follow Him together.

If the disciples needed training to do "us," we do too.

Scripture shows us unity without pretending

The early church had disagreements. Real ones.

In Acts 15, leaders wrestled through a major conflict about requirements for Gentile believers. The conversation wasn't casual. It mattered.

But what's beautiful is what they did with the tension: they talked, they listened, they tested what was being said against God's work, and they made a decision for the sake of unity and mission (Acts 15:1–31, NIV).

They didn't demand everyone feel the same. They fought to stay connected while they worked toward clarity.

Paul also speaks to everyday disagreements—opinions, convictions, and personal practices—and he gives a simple instruction: "Accept one another" (Romans 15:7, NIV).

That word accept doesn't mean approve of everything. It means make room for people. Stop treating difference like disqualification.

Unity isn't built by pretending there are no differences. Unity is built by honoring each other while you sort the differences out.

Three levels of difference

Here's a simple way to keep the "agreement" question from hijacking your relationships. Not all differences are the same kind of difference.

Try sorting tension into three levels:

- Main thing differences (values, integrity, mutual respect): these determine whether connection is healthy and safe.
- Mission differences (purpose, goals, priorities): these determine whether you can move in the same direction.

- Method differences (preferences, style, personality, pace): these determine how you get there.

A lot of conflict happens when we treat a method difference like it's a main thing difference.

We assume a different pace means disrespect. We assume a different tone means rejection. We assume a different preference means they don't care.

Sometimes the issue isn't the issue. Sometimes the issue is the story we're telling ourselves about the issue.

A quick translation that changes everything

When you feel heat rising, try asking yourself: "Is this a main thing, a mission thing, or a method thing?"

If it's a method thing, you can breathe. You can negotiate. You can trade. You can learn.

If it's a mission thing, you can clarify direction and expectations.

If it's a main thing, you can stop pretending it's small and start gathering wisdom for what to do next.

This is one of the kindest gifts you can give a relationship: the gift of accurate interpretation.

How to pursue unity when you don't agree

Unity requires skills. Not perfection—skills. Here are five that change the atmosphere fast:

1) Start with honor.

Honor sounds like: "You matter to me." "Your perspective matters." "I'm not trying to win; I'm trying to understand."

2) Name what you share.

If you can find shared values, shared purpose, and shared respect, you have something to build on. (We'll go deeper on this in Chapter 3.)

3) Tell the truth without heat.

Truth doesn't need volume to be powerful. It needs clarity. When your tone gets sharp, your message gets blurry.

4) Ask a question that slows the story down.

Try this: "Help me understand how you got there."

It's hard to stay defensive when someone is genuinely curious.

5) Repair quickly.

If you mis-speak, overreact, shut down, or assume, don't let pride make it worse.

A simple: "That came out wrong—let me try again," can save days of distance.

Try this sentence

"We don't have to agree on everything to stay in honor. Can we stay connected while we sort this out?"

And if you need a second one that helps you slow the moment down:

"Before I assume, help me understand what matters most to you about this."

Optional reflection

1) Where do you tend to confuse unity with agreement—home, friendships, work, or community?

2) Think of a recent conflict. Was it a main thing difference, mission difference, or method difference?

3) What one sentence could you use next time to stay connected while you seek clarity?

Prayer

Father, thank You that You are steady and faithful. Teach me to pursue unity without pretending. Help me to value people more than being right. Give me wisdom to know what matters most, courage to speak the truth with love, and humility to repair quickly when I miss it. Make me a builder of peace—not passive, not performative, but strong in love. In Jesus' name, amen.

Bridge to Chapter 3

Unity is possible when we keep the main thing the main thing. In Chapter 3, we'll name what that "main thing" is—and how to build it in real life: shared values, shared purpose, and shared respect.

Chapter 3: The Main Thing — Shared Values, Shared Purpose, Shared Respect

If you want to build a healthy "us," you need something stronger than matching preferences.

Preferences are fragile. They change with stress, seasons, and circumstances.

Healthy community is built on three sturdier supports: shared values, shared purpose, and shared respect.

This is true in marriage. It's true in parenting. It's true in friendship. It's true in business.

And it's also true in churches, neighborhoods, teams, and any group of humans trying to do life together without losing their mind.

1) Shared values: What we protect

Values are what you guard when pressure hits.

They answer questions like: What matters most to us? What will we not compromise? What kind of people are we becoming?

A shared value doesn't mean you like all the same things. It means you agree on what should be true about the relationship or the culture.

For example, a couple can have different personalities and still share a value like: "We will speak with kindness in our home."

A workplace team can have different styles and still share a value like: "We will solve problems without blaming people."

Scripture gives values language all over the place: "Be kind" (Ephesians 4:32, NIV). "Speak the truth in love" (Ephesians 4:15, NIV). "Above all, love each other deeply" (1 Peter 4:8, NIV).

Values aren't just words. They're how you choose to behave when you're tired.

2) Shared purpose: Why we're together

Purpose is the "why." It's the direction your relationships are moving.

In a marriage, purpose may include covenant, family, spiritual growth, and building a life together.

In friendships, purpose may include encouragement, fun, honesty, and mutual sharpening.

In a workplace, purpose is often mission-centered: serve customers, build excellence, create value, provide stability, make impact.

When purpose is shared, you can disagree on method and still move in the same direction.

When purpose isn't shared, you can have great chemistry and still feel constantly frustrated—because you're building different futures.

3) Shared respect: How we treat each other

Respect is the atmosphere. It's the tone. It's the way we speak, listen, disagree, and repair.

Respect doesn't require you to feel warm and fuzzy every day. It requires you to stay in honor.

And honor is deeply biblical: "Honor one another above yourselves" (Romans 12:10, NIV).

Respect is what makes truth safe.

It's what allows people to bring their ideas, their concerns, and their differences without fear of humiliation.

It's also what keeps boundaries clean—because you're not trying to punish each other. You're trying to protect what's healthy.

Why these three matter more than personality

Personality tools can be helpful. They give vocabulary. They help you stop personalizing differences.

But tools can't replace values, purpose, and respect.

You can be married to the most "compatible" personality type on paper and still destroy each other if there is no respect.

You can hire a team that looks perfect on a spreadsheet and still create toxicity if there is no shared culture.

The main thing is what holds the "us" together when feelings fluctuate and stress gets loud.

A quick assessment: do we have a main thing?

Here's a practical way to evaluate any relationship or environment without spiraling into judgment.

Ask three simple questions:

- Do we share values we're willing to live out—especially under pressure?
- Do we share a purpose we're actually moving toward?

- Do we share respect—a mutual willingness to honor, listen, and repair?

If the answer is yes, you have something to build on—even if the process is messy.

If the answer is no, don't panic. But don't ignore it either.

Families are built on more than preferences. Friendships are built on more than matching opinions. Work teams are built on more than identical personalities. They're built on shared values, shared purpose, and shared respect.

And when you can't find any shared main thing—when there is no mutual respect, no mutual value, no mutual willingness to honor—that's information. And wise people let that information guide their next steps.

Building the main thing (without making it heavy)

Some people love a worksheet. Most people love a nap.

So here's a simple, low-drama way to build the main thing without turning life into homework: pick one value, one purpose statement, and one respect practice. Start small.

One value: "In this home, we speak with kindness."

One purpose: "We are building a peaceful, truthful family culture."

One respect practice: "When we get heated, we pause and come back with clean words."

That's not a contract. It's a direction.

And direction changes a lot over time.

Try this sentence

"Can we name what matters most to both of us—so we stop fighting about the method and start aligning around the main thing?"

And for teams (home or work):

"What do we want to be true about us when we're under pressure?"

Optional reflection

1) What is one value you want to protect in your closest relationships (kindness, honesty, steadiness, generosity, growth, peace)?

2) What is one purpose you're trying to build toward right now?

3) What is one respect practice that would change the atmosphere immediately (listen fully, no sarcasm, repair quickly, ask questions first)?

Prayer

Father, thank You for making us for connection. Give me wisdom to build the main thing with the people You've placed in my life. Help me choose values that reflect You, pursue purpose that brings life, and practice respect that makes room for growth. Teach me to build healthy culture at home and everywhere I go. In Jesus' name, amen.

Bridge to Chapter 4

Now that we've named the foundation—values, purpose, and respect—we're ready for the first practice that makes it real: honor. In Chapter 4, we'll learn how to start conversations and build culture from dignity instead of defensiveness.

Chapter 4: Honor First — Dignity Is the Starting Line

If you want to build a healthy "us," you have to decide what you believe about people before they act the way you want them to.

Honor isn't a reward for good behavior. Honor is a starting line.

It's the decision that says, "You are made in God's image. You have value. You are worth treating with dignity—right now."

Honor doesn't mean you ignore problems. Honor means you address problems without reducing a person to a problem.

It's the difference between, "You're irresponsible," and, "We need a plan so we can follow through."

Same issue. Different spirit. One attacks identity. The other protects relationship while telling the truth.

What honor is (and what it isn't)

Honor is not flattery. It's not people-pleasing. It's not pretending everything is fine.

Honor is clarity with kindness. It's truth without contempt. It's dignity without denial.

In Scripture language, it looks like "be devoted to one another in love" and "honor one another above yourselves" (Romans 12:10, NIV).

Honor also has backbone.

Jesus is the perfect picture. He could be tender with the broken and direct with the proud. He never shamed people for being human.

But He also didn't let manipulation run the room. Honor isn't weakness. Honor is strength under control.

Why honor changes everything fast

Most conflict escalates because we stop feeling safe.

When people don't feel safe, they defend. When they defend, they interpret. When they interpret, they accuse. And then we're off to the races.

Honor interrupts that cycle. It says, "I'm not your enemy."

Honor is how you keep a hard conversation from becoming a personal war.

And if you're thinking, "But what if they don't honor me back?"—we'll talk about that. Honor doesn't require you to stay in harm.

Honor means you don't become what hurt you.

Two kinds of honor language

In real life, honor usually sounds like one of these two things:

- A value statement: "You matter to me. This matters to me. We matter to me."
- A curiosity question: "Help me understand what's happening for you."

Value statements keep the relationship in the room.

Curiosity questions slow down the story we're tempted to tell about each other.

A quick example: same moment, two starting lines

Let's take something simple: you ask for help, and the other person doesn't follow through.

Starting line without honor sounds like: "You never listen." "You don't care." "I can't rely on you."

Starting line with honor sounds like: "I know you don't mean to leave me carrying this alone. Can we talk about what happened?"

Honor doesn't guarantee agreement. But it greatly increases the odds of understanding.

And understanding is where solutions become possible.

Honor isn't agreement—it's atmosphere

Honor doesn't mean you endorse everything the other person thinks or does.

It means you refuse to use shame as a tool. Shame may create compliance for a moment, but it kills connection over time.

God's kindness leads us to repentance (Romans 2:4, NIV). If kindness is His pathway, it should be ours too.

Try this sentence

"I want to talk about this, and I want to do it with honor—because you matter to me. Can we slow down and work through it?"

And if you need a short reset in the middle of heat:

"I'm for you. I'm not against you. I just want us to be healthy."

Optional reflection

1) When you feel tense, what is your default: attack, withdraw, fix, or please?

2) What would honor look like in your default mode—one notch kinder, one notch clearer?

3) Who do you honor easily? Who is harder? What story might be driving that gap?

Prayer

Father, teach me to start with honor. Help me see people the way You see them—full of value, full of potential, and worthy of dignity. Give me clean words, a steady tone, and courage to tell the truth with love. Make me strong enough to be kind. In Jesus' name, amen.

Bridge to Chapter 5

Honor creates the atmosphere. Now we need a skill that works inside that atmosphere: translation. In Chapter 5, we'll learn how to stop mind-reading, start asking better questions, and translate differences without accusation.

Chapter 5: Translation Language — Curiosity Before Conclusions

If honor is the starting line, translation is the skill that keeps you from tripping over your assumptions.

Most relational damage doesn't begin with evil intent. It begins with misinterpretation.

We see someone's behavior and we attach a motive. We hear a tone and we write a story. We notice a pattern and we label a person.

Translation slows that down and asks, "What else could be true?"

The problem with mind-reading

Mind-reading sounds spiritual sometimes. It isn't. It's usually fear dressed up as certainty.

We assume because it gives us a sense of control. If I can explain you, I can protect myself from being surprised by you.

But assumptions are expensive. They cost trust. They cost joy. They cost connection.

Proverbs says it plainly: "The one who gives an answer before he listens—this is foolishness and disgrace for him" (Proverbs 18:13, CSB).

In other words: don't decide before you understand.

Translation asks: what are you trying to protect?

One of the most helpful questions in this whole book is this: "What are you trying to protect right now?"

When people get defensive, something feels threatened. That's often when the shadow self shows up.

Not because the person is bad—but because they're human.

Defensiveness is usually protecting something tender:

- their dignity (I don't want to feel stupid)
- their safety (I don't feel emotionally safe right now)
- their value (I don't want to feel dismissed)
- their control (I feel anxious when things are uncertain)
- their belonging (I don't want to be left out)

Translation doesn't excuse harmful behavior. It explains the heat so you can choose a wiser response.

It helps you stay curious without becoming naïve.

From accusation to translation

Here's a simple pattern you can use almost anywhere:

1) Name what you value.

2) Name the gap without accusation.

3) Ask a question that invites clarity.

For example:

"I value teamwork. And I'm feeling alone in this. Can you help me understand what happened?"

Or: "I value peace in our home. And our tone got sharp. What do we need right now to reset?"

When you name the good first, you keep the conversation anchored in respect—even when you're naming a gap.

A word for the person who feels 'othered'

If you're the person who often feels misunderstood, overlooked, judged, or 'othered'—treated like an outsider—hear this: Jesus sees you. Fully. Kindly. Clearly.

And He doesn't ask you to earn dignity. He gives it.

So as we learn translation language, don't just use it on other people. Use it on yourself too.

Instead of saying, “I’m too much,” try: “Something in me is trying to protect my heart. What do I need to feel safe and honest?”

Try this sentence

“Before I assume, let me translate: what are you trying to protect right now?”

OR

“Help me understand how you got there.”

A quick self-check: when a tool is helping vs. hurting

Translation language can be supported by tools (personality frameworks, communication models, even simple checklists).

But tools can also be misused. A tool is helping when it produces more:

- patience
- understanding
- honor language
- clear boundaries
- better teamwork

A tool is hurting when it produces more:

- superiority (I'm better than you)
- excuses (I can't help it—I'm a type)
- sarcasm or contempt
- stereotyping
- division

There is a confidence that comes from walking with God—steady, peaceful, clear. That's not arrogance. That's alignment.

The warning sign is when a tool produces comparison instead of compassion, or labels instead of love.

Optional reflection

Think of one relationship that feels stuck.

1) What difference keeps showing up?

2) What might that difference be protecting?

3) What one sentence could you use this week to translate instead of accuse?

Prayer

Father, thank You for the creativity of Your design. Give me wisdom to use tools as mirrors, not masks—vocabulary, not verdicts. Keep my heart grateful and humble, my words life-giving, and my relationships full of honor. Teach me to recognize Your workmanship in others and to work with it, not against it. In Jesus' name, amen.

Bridge to Chapter 6

Now that we have honor and translation language, we're ready for the next practice that makes community sustainable: shared rhythms—how we communicate, plan, and move through life so everyone can breathe.

Chapter 6: Shared Rhythms — How We Communicate So Everyone Can Breathe

Some relationships don't fall apart because people don't love each other.

They fall apart because there's no rhythm—no shared way to communicate, plan, decide, or reset.

So life turns into a constant game of catch-up, with everyone exhausted and nobody feeling truly seen.

Shared rhythms are not boring. Shared rhythms are mercy.

They create enough structure that love can breathe—especially when life gets loud.

Rhythm is a spiritual idea, not just a practical one

Scripture is full of rhythm. Day and night. Work and rest. Seedtime and harvest.

Ecclesiastes says there is "a time for everything" (Ecclesiastes 3:1, NIV). That's rhythm language.

And Jesus lived with rhythm too. He loved people deeply—and He also withdrew to pray and reset (see Mark 1:35, NIV).

He was not ruled by urgency. He was led by the Father.

If you've ever felt guilty because you need quiet, or guilty because you need connection—hear me: rhythm is part of design.

Some people recharge alone. Some people recharge with people. Many of us need a little of both.

The goal is not to force everyone into one style. The goal is to build a rhythm that honors real humans.

Why shared rhythms reduce conflict

Without shared rhythms, we tend to interpret each other's wiring as a personal statement.

The list person thinks the spontaneous person is irresponsible.

The spontaneous person thinks the list person is controlling.

The quick processor thinks the reflective person is avoiding.

The reflective person thinks the quick processor is harsh.

Half the time, what we're calling "attitude" is simply "pace."

Shared rhythms reduce that misinterpretation. They give you a shared container.

Instead of constantly negotiating life in the heat of the moment, you pre-decide some things in peace.

The four rhythms every "us" needs

Whether you're building a marriage, family culture, friendship circle, or team, these four rhythms will change the atmosphere fast:

- Connection rhythm: when and how we connect
- Communication rhythm: how we talk when things are normal—and when they're tense
- Planning rhythm: how we handle schedules, tasks, and expectations
- Repair rhythm: how we reset after conflict or miscommunication

Let's make these practical.

1) Connection rhythm: how we stay close

Connection rhythm answers: How do we stay emotionally connected in the middle of real life?

For some people, connection happens naturally in conversation.

For others, connection happens while doing something side-by-side—walking, working, driving, cooking.

And for some, connection is easier in small doses than in long marathons.

A simple connection rhythm can look like:

- Ten minutes of presence before tasks (phones down, eyes up)
- A weekly check-in: "How are we—really?"
- A monthly 'reset' conversation: what's working, what's heavy, what needs to change

Connection is not measured by constant togetherness. It's measured by meaningful attentiveness.

2) Communication rhythm: how we talk

Communication rhythm answers: When something matters, how do we talk about it?

Here are three agreements that keep communication healthy:

- We don't do important conversations while escalated.
- We ask questions before we write stories.
- We use clean words—truth without contempt.

Paul says, “Let no unwholesome talk come out of your mouths, but only what is helpful for building others up” (Ephesians 4:29, NIV).

That verse doesn’t mean you avoid hard truth. It means your words are meant to build, not burn.

A practical communication rhythm can be as simple as:

“If it’s important, we schedule it.”

That one sentence saves a lot of damage—because it keeps serious conversations from happening in the doorway, the car, or over a half-heated text message.

3) Planning rhythm: how we handle life logistics

Planning rhythm answers: How do we prevent the ‘I thought you were doing it’ problem?

This is where so many good-hearted people get into avoidable conflict.

Not because they don’t care—but because expectations weren’t made clear.

Some people feel loved by spontaneity. Others feel loved by preparedness.

Neither is sinful. Both can be beautiful. But when you combine them, you need rhythm.

A planning rhythm can look like:

- One shared calendar (yes, really)
- A weekly 'what's coming' review
- A simple division of responsibility: "You own this; I own that"
- A phrase you repeat often: "Let's get it out of our heads and onto a plan"

In business language, that's stewardship. In family language, that's peace.

And Scripture has room for this. Paul even says, "Let everything be done in a fitting and orderly way" (1 Corinthians 14:40, NIV).

Order isn't a personality type. It's a kindness when people share a life.

4) Repair rhythm: how we reset

Repair rhythm answers: When we miss it—how do we come back?

Healthy people don't avoid conflict. Healthy people repair.

A repair rhythm keeps small moments from becoming long seasons of distance.

A repair rhythm can be:

- Name it: "That didn't come out the way I meant."
- Own it: "I was sharp / I shut down / I assumed."
- Reframe it: "Here's what I was trying to protect."
- Re-connect: "I'm for you. Let's reset."

This is where humility becomes a superpower.

"Clothe yourselves with compassion, kindness, humility, gentleness and patience" (Colossians 3:12, NIV).

That's not poetic decoration. That's relational oxygen.

When rhythm feels like control

Let's name a real fear: some people hear "rhythm" and think "control."

If you've lived with controlling people, structure can feel threatening.

But healthy rhythm isn't control—it's clarity.

Control says, "Do it my way."

Rhythm says, "Let's build a way that works for us."

And if you're the person who loves structure, remember: rhythm is meant to serve love, not replace it.

If you're the person who loves flexibility, remember: rhythm is meant to protect peace, not kill joy.

The win is not "my preference wins." The win is "our life works."

Try this sentence

"Can we build a simple rhythm for this so we stop re-fighting the same problem?"

And for connection, specifically:

"I don't need a perfect plan—I just need a predictable moment of you."

Optional reflection

1) Which rhythm is missing most right now: connection, communication, planning, or repair?

2) What is one simple rhythm you could try for two weeks (not forever—just two weeks)?

3) What resistance do you feel about rhythm—and what might that resistance be protecting?

Prayer

Father, thank You that You are a God of peace, not confusion. Teach us to build rhythms that serve love and honor design. Give us wisdom to communicate clearly, plan kindly, and repair quickly. Help our 'us' become a place where people can breathe. In Jesus' name, amen.

Bridge to Chapter 7

Rhythm makes life workable. Next, we need clarity about decisions—because nothing triggers drama faster than unclear 'who decides what.' In Chapter 7, we'll build a simple decision framework that keeps relationships strong and teams healthy.

Chapter 7: Decision-Making Without Drama — Roles, Clarity, and Clean 'Yes/No'

If you want to see where a relationship or a team gets stressed fast, watch how decisions get made.

Or don't get made.

Unclear decisions create confusion. Confusion creates frustration. Frustration creates blame.

And blame is the fastest way to turn an "us" into an "us vs. them."

The goal isn't to remove emotion from decisions. The goal is to remove fog.

Clarity is kindness.

God cares about leadership, not chaos

In Exodus 18, Moses is doing too much. He's exhausted, and the people are waiting in long lines for help.

His father-in-law, Jethro, gives him a wisdom bomb: "What you are doing is not good" (Exodus 18:17, NIV).

Then he tells Moses to share responsibility—appoint leaders, distribute decision-making, and create a workable system.

That is not corporate. That is biblical stewardship.

Later, in Acts 6, the early church faces a practical conflict about fair distribution. The apostles don't ignore it. They don't micromanage it either.

They clarify roles and empower others to solve it, so the mission stays strong (Acts 6:1–7, NIV).

Healthy community requires clear roles and shared responsibility.

Three kinds of decisions

One reason decisions get messy is because we treat every decision like the same kind of decision.

Try sorting decisions into three categories:

- Everyday decisions (low impact): meals, errands, schedules, routine purchases
- Directional decisions (medium impact): budgets, parenting approaches, staffing, boundaries, commitments
- Destiny decisions (high impact): marriage covenants, major moves, business partnerships, calling assignments

Everyday decisions should not require a three-hour meeting. (That's a sign we need snacks and a nap.)

Directional decisions require conversation and clarity.

Destiny decisions require prayer, counsel, and time—because they shape your future.

A simple framework: Decide, Advise, Inform

Here's a framework that works in homes and workplaces:

For any decision, clarify three things:

- Who decides? (the decider)
- Who advises? (the voices that must be heard before deciding)
- Who is informed? (the people who need to know once it's decided)

This removes so much drama.

If everyone thinks they're the decider, you get power struggles.

If no one is the decider, you get drift.

If the wrong people are consulted, you get resentment.

But when roles are clear, people can participate without fighting for control.

Decision clarity in marriage and family

In marriage, decision-making is ideally shared. But even shared decisions need roles.

For example: if one person handles finances day-to-day, they may be the 'decider' on everyday purchases—while both are advisers on budget direction.

If one person manages schedules, they may be the 'decider' on calendar logistics—while both are advisers on priority commitments.

The goal is not domination. The goal is teamwork.

And if you're a parent, clarity gets even more important.

Children don't feel safe in chaos. They may not articulate it, but they feel it.

A united, clear parental decision—even if it's not perfect—is often kinder than two parents competing for control.

Decision clarity in teams and workplaces

In teams, unclear decision rights create silent sabotage.

People nod in meetings and complain in hallways.

Or they slow-walk implementation because they never truly bought in.

Clarity prevents that.

A healthy leader doesn't have to be the smartest person in the room. They have to be the clearest.

Proverbs says, "Plans fail for lack of counsel, but with many advisers they succeed" (Proverbs 15:22, NIV).

Notice the balance: counsel matters, but somebody still has to decide.

Unity is not everyone getting their way. Unity is everyone staying in honor while moving forward together.

Clean 'yes' and clean 'no'

Jesus gives us one of the most practical leadership principles in a single phrase: "Let your 'Yes' be 'Yes,' and your 'No,' 'No'" (Matthew 5:37, NIV).

That's integrity language.

A clean yes means you can follow through without resentment.

A clean no means you can stay honest without guilt-tripping yourself—or punishing others.

A lot of drama comes from unclear yes/no.

We say yes to keep peace, then we feel used.

We say no in a sharp tone, then we feel distant.

Clean yes/no is a skill—and it protects relationships.

Try this sentence

"Before we decide, can we clarify: who is the decider, who needs to be consulted, and who just needs to be informed?"

And for boundaries around yes/no:

"I can say yes to this if we can also say no to that."

Optional reflection

1) Where do decisions create the most tension—home, friendships, work, or community?

2) Is the tension coming from unclear roles, unclear purpose, or unclear yes/no?

3) What is one decision you could clarify this week using Decide / Advise / Inform?

Prayer

Father, thank You for wisdom that makes life workable. Help me lead with clarity and humility. Give me courage to say clean yes and clean no. Teach me to invite counsel without losing direction, and to keep unity without demanding sameness. Make our relationships steady and our decisions full of peace. In Jesus' name, amen.

Bridge to Chapter 8

Now that we have shared rhythms and decision clarity, we're ready to talk about conflict—because even healthy people disagree. In Chapter 8, we'll learn how to do conflict in a way that builds instead of breaks: truth with love, and without heat.

Chapter 8: Conflict That Builds — Truth With Love (and Without Heat)

If you put two humans in a room long enough, conflict will happen.

Not because you're failing. Because you're alive.

The question is not whether you will have conflict. The question is whether your conflict will build you—or break you.

A lot of us grew up with one of two models:

- Explode: raise the volume, win the argument, prove the point.
- Avoid: stay quiet, keep the peace, swallow the truth, carry the resentment.

Neither one is the Jesus way.

Jesus doesn't ask us to avoid truth. And He doesn't teach us to use truth as a weapon.

He teaches us to tell the truth in love (Ephesians 4:15, NIV). That's a skill—and it can be learned.

Why conflict gets hot so fast

Conflict gets hot when it stops being about the issue and starts being about identity.

We don't just hear, "We need to talk about the budget." We hear, "You don't trust me."

We don't just hear, "That tone hurt." We hear, "You think I'm a bad person."

And then our nervous system does what nervous systems do: it protects.

That's why we keep circling back to translation: what are you trying to protect right now?

James gives one of the most practical conflict instructions in Scripture: be "quick to listen, slow to speak and slow to become angry" (James 1:19, NIV).

That's not a personality preference. That's a wisdom path.

Truth without heat: the goal

I call it truth without heat.

Not truth without backbone. Not truth without clarity. Truth without heat.

Heat makes people defend. Defense makes people stop listening.

If the goal is connection and clarity, we need truth that invites listening.

Proverbs says, "A gentle answer turns away wrath" (Proverbs 15:1, NIV).

Gentle doesn't mean weak. Gentle means controlled.

It means you have enough strength to keep your tone from doing damage.

The Clean Conflict Map

Here's a simple map you can use in marriage, parenting, friendships, and teams. I call it Clean Conflict:

1) Regulate

2) Honor

3) Name the gap

4) Ask for the next right step

Step 1: Regulate before you communicate

If your body is flooded, your words won't be clean.

So the first step is sometimes not a sentence—it's a pause.

A pause can sound like: “I want to talk about this, but I’m not in a good tone right now. Can we take ten minutes and come back?”

That’s not avoidance. That’s wisdom.

A regulated person can listen. A flooded person can only react.

If you need a simple boundary for yourself, try this: don’t do important conversations when you’re hungry, exhausted, or already escalated.

Step 2: Start with honor

Honor keeps the conversation inside dignity. It sounds like: “You matter to me.” “We matter to me.” “I’m for you.”

It reminds the other person: this is not a courtroom. This is a relationship.

Step 3: Name the gap without accusation

Accusation attacks a person. Naming a gap addresses a moment.

Accusation sounds like: “You always…” “You never…” “You’re just like…”

Naming a gap sounds like:

- “And I need us to do this together.”

- “And I need a few minutes of presence before we jump into tasks.”
- “And I need a plan so I don’t feel overwhelmed.”

When you name the good first, you keep the conversation anchored in respect—even when you’re naming a gap.

Step 4: Ask for the next right step

Healthy conflict doesn’t just vent; it moves.

It asks, “What do we do from here?”

Try questions like: “What would help you feel supported?” “What would make this workable?” “What do you need from me right now?”

Jesus gives a practical conflict pathway too: go directly to the person (Matthew 18:15, NIV).

Not to the group chat. Not to your favorite listener. Not to your inner jury.

Direct conversations—done with honor—protect relationships and prevent unnecessary fallout.

A quick example: workplace conflict that builds

Picture a team where the big-picture person moves fast and the detail-first person slows things down.

Without honor, the fast person calls the other "negative," and the detail person calls the fast one "careless."

With clean conflict, the conversation shifts.

"I value accuracy. And I also value momentum. Can we agree on what 'good enough' looks like for this stage of the project?"

That one sentence turns a clash into a collaboration.

Try this sentence

"I'm not trying to win—I'm trying to understand and build something healthy. Can we talk about this with clean words?"

And if you need a quick de-escalator:

"I hear you. Give me a second to take that in."

Optional reflection

1) Which conflict default do you lean toward—explode or avoid?

2) What does your body do when you feel threatened (tight chest, fast words, shutting down, sarcasm, silence)?

3) What would "truth without heat" look like in one conversation you need to have this week?

Prayer

Father, teach me to tell the truth with love. Give me wisdom to pause when I'm flooded, courage to speak when I'm afraid, and humility to listen when I want to defend. Help my words build instead of burn. Make me a peacemaker with backbone. In Jesus' name, amen.

Bridge to Chapter 9

Clean conflict keeps the relationship in the room. Next, we need a skill that protects the "us" over time: quick repair—how to reset fast so small gaps don't become canyons.

Chapter 9: Quick Repair — How to Reset Before the Gap Becomes a Canyon

Most relationships don't break in one moment.

They break in a thousand small moments that never get repaired.

A sharp tone that stays unowned. A misunderstood comment that becomes a story. A disappointment that turns into distance.

That's why repair is one of the most important skills in any healthy "us."

Repair doesn't mean you never miss it. It means you don't stay stuck in it.

Repair is how love stays breathable.

Why repair is hard (and holy)

Repair requires humility—because someone has to go first.

And pride loves to say, "Well, I wouldn't have said it if you hadn't…"

But God's way is different.

Scripture says, “Do not let the sun go down while you are still angry” (Ephesians 4:26, NIV).

That doesn’t mean you fix everything by bedtime like a sitcom.

It means you don’t let anger camp in your house and call it a roommate.

Quick repair doesn’t erase the issue. It protects the relationship while you work on the issue.

The Repair Loop: four simple moves

Here’s a simple repair loop you can use almost anywhere:

1) Name it

2) Own it

3) Rebuild

4) Reconnect

1) Name it

Name the moment without defending it.

“That came out sharp.”

“I shut down.”

“I assumed the worst.”

"We got heated."

2) Own it

Ownership is the opposite of blame-shifting.

It sounds like: "That's on me." "I can see how that landed." "I don't want to talk to you like that."

You don't have to confess things you didn't do. But you can own your part cleanly.

3) Rebuild

Rebuild is where you clarify what you meant—or what you need—and ask for a better way forward.

"What I was trying to say is…"

"What I need is…"

"Can we try that again?"

This is also where your favorite translation question can help.

If the moment got defensive, try: "What were you trying to protect right then? And here's what I was trying to protect…"

That doesn't excuse the behavior. It explains the heat so the next time can be wiser.

4) Reconnect

Reconnection is the relational re-set.

It's where you remind each other: we're still us.

"I'm for you."

"I love you."

"We're okay. We're learning."

Sometimes reconnection is a hug. Sometimes it's a walk. Sometimes it's simply sitting down again with softer eyes.

The point is this: you don't leave the relationship in the cold.

Apology language that actually heals

A strong apology has three parts:

- Impact: "I can see that hurt you."
- Ownership: "I was wrong / I was out of line."
- Change: "Here's what I'll do differently."

Avoid the kind of apology that keeps you in charge: "I'm sorry you feel that way."

That's not repair. That's a polite dismissal.

A healing apology sounds like: "I'm sorry I spoke to you with contempt. That's not who I want to be. I'm going to slow down next time."

Quick repair is not quick trust

Repair restores connection. Trust is rebuilt over time.

So if note-taking is your natural wiring, you can relax: you don't have to decide the entire future of a relationship in one moment.

Repair is a step. Trust is a process.

And if you're the forgiving type who reconnects quickly, remember: healthy repair still includes clarity and boundaries.

Forgiveness can be immediate. Rebuilding trust is usually gradual. Both can be true.

Try this sentence

"That didn't come out the way I meant. Can I try again—with cleaner words?"

And if you need a short version that works anywhere:

"I'm sorry. I own that. I'm for you."

Optional reflection

1) What is your default after conflict—repair quickly, withdraw, justify, or punish with distance?

2) Think of one relationship where small moments have piled up. What is one repair you could initiate this week?

3) What sentence would make it easier for you to go first?

Prayer

Father, make me quick to repent and quick to repair. Give me humility to own my part and courage to tell the truth with love. Teach me to be a safe person—honest, kind, and willing to begin again. Heal what needs healing and strengthen what needs strengthening. In Jesus' name, amen.

Bridge to Chapter 10

Now that we can repair, we're ready for the boundaries that keep community sustainable. In Chapter 10, we'll talk about boundaries that bless—clarity without bitterness.

Chapter 10: Boundaries That Bless — Clarity Without Bitterness

If love is going to last, it needs clarity.

That's what boundaries give you—not walls, not punishments, not silent treatment—clarity.

A boundary is simply a loving line that protects what's healthy and names what's not.

Some of us hear the word boundaries and feel relief.

Others hear it and feel fear—because boundaries have been used against us before.

So let's define it clearly:

Boundaries are not about controlling other people. They're about owning your choices and your responsibilities.

Jesus had boundaries

If you've ever thought boundaries feel unspiritual, look at Jesus.

He loved people completely—and He didn't say yes to every demand.

He withdrew to pray. He walked away from crowds. He set timing. He said no. He said not yet.

He did not confuse compassion with access.

That is one of the most freeing things you can learn: love doesn't require unlimited availability.

Even in ministry, Jesus sometimes didn't engage.

He asked questions. He told stories. He moved on when people wanted a spectacle.

His boundaries protected His mission and kept Him aligned with the Father.

What boundaries protect

Boundaries protect:

- your peace
- your values
- your responsibilities
- your relationships
- your capacity
- your calling

A boundary is what keeps you from living in constant resentment.

Resentment is often a signal that a boundary is needed—because you've been saying yes when you should have been saying no.

Two common boundary mistakes

Most boundary problems fall into two ditches:

- No boundaries: over-giving, over-explaining, over-functioning, then exploding or shutting down.
- Hard boundaries: cutting off, punishing, or using distance as a weapon.

Healthy boundaries live in the middle: clear, kind, consistent.

A boundary isn't a threat; it's a truth

A threat sounds like: "If you do that again, I'm done with you."

A boundary sounds like: "If this continues, I will need to step back to protect what's healthy."

One is punishment. The other is clarity.

And clarity can be deeply loving—because it gives people the dignity of knowing what's real.

Boundaries without bitterness

Bitterness happens when we use boundaries as a way to keep the other person guilty.

Healthy boundaries aren't revenge. They're stewardship.

They say: "I'm going to guard my heart, my home, my peace, and my calling—and I'm going to do it with clean hands."

Scripture says, "Above all else, guard your heart" (Proverbs 4:23, NIV).

Guarding your heart doesn't mean closing it off. It means protecting it from what would poison it.

What a healthy boundary sounds like

Here are some boundary sentences that keep your tone clean:

- "I can do this, but not that."
- "I'm not available for that conversation when we're heated. I'm available when we can speak with respect."
- "If you raise your voice at me, I will pause and come back when we can talk calmly."
- "I care about you, and I'm not able to carry this alone."
- "I'm willing to work on this with you. I'm not willing to do it without mutual respect."

Notice the pattern: boundaries don't try to force the other person to change. They simply name what you will do with clarity.

When there is no shared main thing

Families are built on more than preferences. Friendships are built on more than matching opinions. Work teams are built on more than identical personalities.

They're built on shared values, shared purpose, and shared respect.

And when you can't find any shared main thing—when there is no mutual respect, no mutual value, no mutual willingness to honor—that's information. And wise people let that information guide their next steps.

Sometimes the next step is a hard conversation.

Sometimes it's a boundary.

Sometimes it's a season of distance.

And sometimes, sadly, it's acknowledging that a relationship cannot be close until respect exists.

This is where we keep our hearts clean.

We don't demonize. We don't gossip. We don't punish.

We become wise.

Try this sentence

"I'm committed to being respectful. And I need our connection to be respectful too. If we can't do that right now, I'm going to step back and we can revisit this later."

And for people-pleasers who need a clean no:

"I can't say yes to that, and I'm not angry about it. It's just not mine to carry."

Optional reflection

1) Where are you feeling resentment—what might it be telling you about a boundary you need?

2) What boundary would protect your peace without punishing someone else?

3) What fear rises up when you think about setting that boundary (rejection, conflict, guilt)? What might that fear be protecting?

Prayer

Father, give me wisdom and courage to set boundaries with clean hands and a soft heart. Help me to guard what You've entrusted to me—my peace, my home, my calling—without bitterness. Teach me to speak truth with love and to stay in honor even when I have to step back. In Jesus' name, amen.

Bridge to Chapter 11

Boundaries protect the 'us.' Next, we're going to talk about belonging—how to include people and build community without losing yourself.

Chapter 11: Belonging — How to Include People Without Losing Yourself

Belonging is one of the deepest longings in the human heart.

We want to be known—and still wanted.

We want to be included without having to perform.

And we want to be different without being treated like an outsider.

Healthy community doesn't demand sameness. It creates belonging.

But belonging isn't the same as access.

Belonging is love. Access is trust. And trust is built over time.

Jesus made room for people

Jesus had a remarkable way of seeing people.

He looked at the overlooked. He touched the untouchable. He ate with the outcast.

He didn't wait for people to earn dignity. He gave it.

That's why so many people who felt rejected ran toward Him.

When you create belonging, you are echoing the heart of God.

You are saying, "There's room for you here."

Belonging starts with presence

In a distracted world, presence is a spiritual gift.

Belonging begins when someone feels seen.

Not fixed. Not managed. Seen.

Presence doesn't require hours. It requires attention.

A person can feel deeply valued in five minutes if you are fully there.

And a person can feel lonely in a room full of people if no one is truly paying attention.

Inclusion without over-functioning

Some of us try to create belonging by over-functioning.

We carry the emotional load. We keep the peace. We anticipate needs. We manage the vibe.

But if belonging depends on one person doing all the work, that community will eventually collapse—usually into resentment.

Belonging is healthiest when responsibility is shared.

A mature 'us' doesn't require one person to become the glue. It invites everyone to contribute.

Belonging also needs boundaries

This is where we tell the truth: some people use the language of belonging to demand unhealthy access.

They want closeness without respect. Connection without accountability.

But love doesn't require you to abandon wisdom.

You can create belonging and still have limits.

You can be kind and still say no.

You can include people and still protect your home, your peace, and your calling.

A simple belonging practice: widen the circle

One of the easiest ways to build belonging is to widen the circle in small moments:

- Ask an honest question and listen all the way through.
- Use people's names and look them in the eyes.
- Invite someone into the conversation who is being overlooked.

- Celebrate what someone contributes (especially the quiet contributors).
- Make room for different styles—different 'lenses'—without mocking them.

Belonging is built through small repeated signals: "You matter. You're safe. There's room."

Belonging language that creates safety

Try phrases like:

- "I'm glad you're here."
- "Your perspective matters."
- "I may not see it the same way, but I want to understand you."
- "You don't have to be like me to belong with me."

That last sentence is worth reading twice.

When you are the one who feels 'outside'

If you're the one who often feels overlooked, misunderstood, or like you don't fit—let me speak to you for a minute.

Your difference isn't a flaw. It's a feature.

You were not created to be a copy. You were created to carry something unique.

And the right community won't require you to shrink to be loved.

Sometimes the wisest thing you can do is stop trying to earn belonging in places that require you to betray your design.

That doesn't mean you leave in anger. It means you leave with wisdom.

God may have something healthier for you—people who can honor your wiring and welcome your contribution.

Try this sentence

"I want to belong here, and I also want to be honest about what I need to stay healthy. Can we talk about what belonging looks like for both of us?"

And if you need a gentle boundary inside inclusion:

"I care about you, and I'm not able to do that. Here's what I can do."

Optional reflection

1) Where do you feel the most belonging right now? What makes it safe?

2) Where do you feel the least belonging? What might be missing—presence, respect, shared purpose, shared responsibility?

3) What is one small 'widen the circle' action you could take this week?

Prayer

Father, thank You that You welcome us. Teach me to create belonging the way You do—truthful, kind, and full of honor. Help me to include people without over-functioning, and to set wise limits without closing my heart. Make my life a place where others can breathe and grow. In Jesus' name, amen.

Bridge to Chapter 12

Now that we've built a foundation and core practices, we're going to apply them to the places we live every day—starting with marriage as team.

Chapter 12: Marriage as Team — Two Designs, One Covenant

Marriage will teach you quickly that love is not the same as teamwork.

Most couples start with chemistry—shared laughter, shared dreams, shared attraction.

And then real life shows up with bills, schedules, tired bodies, different childhood stories, and two nervous systems that don't always regulate the same way.

That's not failure. That's marriage becoming real.

If Book 1 helped you name your design, and Book 2 helped you honor the design in others, then marriage is where the "us" gets tested daily.

Two designs. One covenant.

And covenant love isn't just a feeling—it's a choice to build something together, season after season.

The goal isn't sameness; it's unity

A healthy marriage is not two people becoming identical.

It's two people becoming aligned.

That's why Scripture gives us words like "one" without demanding "same."

Jesus said, "the two will become one flesh" (Matthew 19:5, NIV).

Oneness is not personality matching. It's shared direction, shared devotion, and shared honor.

And if you've ever looked at your spouse and thought, "How can one human be so wonderful… and so confusing?" welcome to the club.

Sometimes God gives you a spouse who complements you. Sometimes He gives you a spouse who confronts you—in the best possible way.

Either way, the invitation is the same: learn to build.

Common marriage friction points (and what they're really about)

In coaching, I've seen the same friction points show up again and again. They usually sound like:

- "You don't listen."
- "You're too emotional / not emotional enough."
- "You never help."
- "You're always working."
- "Why can't you just relax / plan / decide / talk?"

But underneath those words, the deeper questions are often:

- "Am I safe with you?"
- "Do I matter to you?"
- "Are we in this together?"
- "Can I trust you with my heart?"

That's why the practices from earlier chapters matter so much here: honor, translation, rhythm, clarity, clean conflict, repair, boundaries, belonging.

Those aren't abstract. They are marriage oxygen.

Build a marriage culture (not just a marriage schedule)

Most couples spend more time talking about what they have to do than how they want to be.

So let's make this simple: every healthy marriage needs a culture. A "how we do us here."

A marriage culture is built on shared values, shared purpose, and shared respect (Chapter 3).

Here are three starter statements that create culture quickly:

- Value: "In this marriage, we speak with kindness—even when we disagree."
- Purpose: "We are building a life that honors God and strengthens each other."
- Respect: "We will not use contempt, sarcasm, or silence as weapons."

Those aren't rules. They are guardrails. They protect love when stress tries to hijack it.

The teamwork triangle: Care, Clarity, Contribution

If you want a simple way to evaluate how your marriage team is doing, try this triangle:

- Care: Do we feel emotionally connected and valued?
- Clarity: Do we have clear expectations and decisions?
- Contribution: Are we carrying life together in a fair, honest way?

When one corner gets weak, resentment usually shows up.

Care without clarity can feel romantic but chaotic.

Clarity without care can feel efficient but cold.

Contribution without both can feel like a business partnership, not a covenant.

A practical rhythm: the 15-minute check-in

You don't need a three-hour relationship summit every week.

Try a 15-minute check-in once a week. Just enough time to keep the "us" healthy.

Here are three questions that keep it simple:

- What felt good between us this week?
- What felt heavy or tense?
- What is one thing we can do next week that would help us feel more connected?

This is not a time to unload every historical frustration. It's a rhythm to keep small gaps from becoming canyons.

If something bigger needs attention, schedule it—don't spring it. (Chapter 6.)

When you're wired differently, translate the difference

Maybe one of you processes out loud and the other processes internally.

Maybe one of you wants a plan and the other wants freedom.

Maybe one of you recharges with people and the other recharges alone.

None of those are sins. They're designs.

But designs under pressure can become shadows.

So don't just argue about the behavior. Translate the need underneath.

Try asking: "What are you trying to protect right now?"

Often the answer is something tender: peace, dignity, control, safety, or belonging.

When you can name what's being protected, you can stop fighting each other and start fighting for each other.

Try this sentence

"I don't want to win this. I want us. Can we slow down and figure out what we're both trying to protect right now?"

And a second one that rebuilds teamwork fast:

"What would 'together' look like for you this week?"

Optional reflection

1) Which corner of the triangle needs attention right now—care, clarity, or contribution?

2) What is one rhythm that would help your marriage breathe (check-in, calendar review, date, prayer, repair practice)?

3) What difference do you tend to personalize—and how could you translate it as design instead?

Prayer

Father, thank You for covenant love. Teach us to build a marriage that reflects You—steady, kind, honest, and strong. Help us honor our differences, translate our stress with wisdom, and repair quickly when we miss it. Make our home a place of peace and belonging. In Jesus' name, amen.

Bridge to Chapter 13

Marriage as team shapes the whole home. Next, we'll talk about parenting with partnership—how to stay united as parents even when your styles differ, and how to create a culture your children can feel.

Chapter 13: Parenting with Partnership — Unity at Home Even When Styles Differ

Parenting will reveal your wiring faster than almost anything else.

If you're more laid back, you'll feel it when your child needs structure.

If you're more structured, you'll feel it when your child needs softness.

And if you're parenting with another adult, you'll feel it when your partner's instincts don't match yours.

Here's the truth: most parents love their kids deeply and still feel overwhelmed.

So let's remove shame right now.

Parenting is not a performance. Parenting is formation—of your children and of you.

Children don't need perfect parents—they need united parents

United doesn't mean identical.

United means your children know the home has a steady center.

It means they don't feel like they're living in two different countries depending on which parent is on duty.

And it means you and your co-parent are committed to teamwork—even when you disagree.

Scripture gives a simple picture of unity and formation: "Train up a child in the way he should go" (Proverbs 22:6, NKJV).

That phrase doesn't mean "control every outcome."

It means create a way—a path, a culture, a direction.

Two parenting lenses are better than one

One of the biggest shifts I've seen in healthy families is when parents stop fighting over who is right and start asking, "What does each of us bring that our children need?"

Because children need more than one lens.

They need tenderness and truth.

They need boundaries and belonging.

They need empathy and responsibility.

They need fun and follow-through.

God is brilliant like that.

Often, one parent is naturally more compassionate and the other is naturally more corrective.

One tends to see the child's heart; the other tends to see the child's habits.

One prioritizes peace; the other prioritizes growth.

Both can be gifts—when they're partnered.

The danger: when stress turns your lens into your shadow

Under pressure, our strengths can become shadows.

The compassionate parent can become permissive because conflict feels threatening.

The corrective parent can become harsh because chaos feels threatening.

The peacemaker can avoid necessary confrontation.

The challenger can confront without warmth.

That's why we keep returning to the question: what are we trying to protect?

When you understand what you're protecting, you can choose maturity instead of reaction.

The parenting huddle (a quick teamwork practice)

I'm going to give you a practice that changes home culture quickly: the parenting huddle.

It's a short, private conversation between parents—before you address a pattern with your child.

It can be five minutes. It can be a text exchange. The point is unity.

In the huddle, ask:

- What is the real issue we're trying to address?
- What value are we protecting (respect, honesty, responsibility, kindness)?
- What does tenderness look like here?
- What does structure look like here?
- What consequence is fair and actually teachable?

This keeps you from correcting your child while also correcting your spouse—at the same time. (And yes, I've seen that go badly.)

The huddle protects the marriage team and the child's sense of safety.

Avoid the 'good cop / bad cop' trap

When parents don't huddle, children naturally learn to navigate the gap.

They ask the permissive parent when they want a yes.

They avoid the stricter parent when they want to dodge consequences.

Then parents end up resenting each other—and the child ends up anxious, because the home feels unpredictable.

Unity doesn't mean you never change your mind. It means you don't make your child carry your disagreement.

If you need to disagree, do it privately. Then come back to your child with one clear message.

Correction without shame

Discipline is meant to teach, not humiliate.

Scripture says, "Fathers, do not exasperate your children; instead, bring them up in the training and instruction of the Lord" (Ephesians 6:4, NIV).

That verse holds both sides: training and instruction, without exasperation.

In other words: firmness with kindness.

A child can learn responsibility without losing dignity.

A child can receive consequences without being shamed.

And a child can be corrected while still feeling deeply loved.

A practical script: the three-part correction

If you need a simple structure for correction that keeps honor intact, try this:

- Connect: "I love you. You matter."
- Correct: "Here's what needs to change."
- Coach: "Here's what we'll do next time."

This mirrors God's heart: He doesn't throw us away when we fail. He trains us. He restores. He leads us forward.

Try this sentence

To your co-parent: "I want our kids to feel steady. Can we huddle for five minutes so we respond as a team?"

To your child (when you need correction with dignity): "I love you. And this behavior isn't okay. Let's talk about what we do next time."

Optional reflection

1) What is your default parenting lens under stress—more permissive or more corrective?

2) What might you be trying to protect (peace, control, respect, safety, dignity)?

3) What would a weekly parenting huddle look like for you—time, place, and one question you always ask?

Prayer

Father, thank You for trusting us with our children. Give us wisdom to parent with unity and love. Help us correct without shaming, and comfort without rescuing. Teach us to build a home where our kids feel safe, seen, and strengthened. And when we miss it, help us repair quickly—with You and with each other. In Jesus' name, amen.

Bridge to Chapter 14

Now that we've built marriage and parenting teamwork, we're going to widen the circle to friendship—how to build circles that are fun, safe, and growth-producing without forcing everyone into the same mold.

Chapter 14: Friendship Circles — Fun Friends, Growth Friends, Safe Friends

Friendship is one of God's most underrated gifts.

It's also one of the most misunderstood.

A lot of people are quietly disappointed in friendship because they're expecting one person to be everything:

the fun friend, the safe friend, the deep friend, the mentor friend, the honest friend, the emergency friend, the adventure friend…

That's a lot to put on one human. (Even the best humans need naps.)

Healthy community usually looks like a circle, not a single point.

Different friendships serve different purposes—and that doesn't mean any of them are "less." It means you're building an "us" that has wisdom.

Scripture assumes we need people

Ecclesiastes says, "Two are better than one… If either of them falls down, one can help the other up" (Ecclesiastes 4:9–10, NIV).

That's not just practical. That's spiritual.

God knows life has seasons when you need someone to help you back to your feet.

Proverbs says, "A friend loves at all times" (Proverbs 17:17, NIV).

And it also says, "As iron sharpens iron, so one person sharpens another" (Proverbs 27:17, NIV).

Notice both themes: comfort and sharpening. Belonging and growth.

Three friendship circles that keep you healthy

Here's a simple framework that helps people build friendships with less confusion and less resentment.

1) Fun friends

Fun friends are the people you laugh with, unwind with, go do life with.

These friendships remind your nervous system that joy is holy. Seriously.

If you're always serious, you'll start treating every conversation like a counseling appointment.

Sometimes you don't need a breakthrough. Sometimes you need tacos and laughter.

2) Safe friends

Safe friends are the people you can be honest with.

They don't punish your vulnerability. They don't weaponize what you share.

They can hold your story with care.

Safe friends don't have to agree with you about everything, but they do have to respect you.

They are the kind of people where you can say, "I'm not okay," and you don't have to manage their reaction.

3) Growth friends

Growth friends are the people who help you become more like Jesus.

They're the ones who can lovingly challenge you.

They ask the question you're avoiding.

They tell you the truth without humiliation.

They are iron-sharpening-iron people. And yes—sometimes they are a little annoying, because growth is rarely convenient.

When you understand these circles, you stop expecting your fun friend to mentor you, and you stop expecting your mentor to be your Friday-night hangout.

You stop being offended by what a friendship isn't—and you start being grateful for what it is.

Biblical examples that bring friendship to life

David and Jonathan are one of the clearest pictures of covenant friendship. Scripture says Jonathan loved David "as he loved himself" (1 Samuel 18:1, NIV).

That's not shallow friendship. That's loyal, courageous, protective friendship.

It's also a picture of honor: Jonathan recognized what God was doing in David, even when it cost him personally.

That's a safe friend and a growth friend in one relationship—rare, but beautiful.

Jesus also models friendship. He had crowds, He had the twelve, and He had a smaller inner circle.

He loved everyone, but He didn't share the same level of access with everyone.

That's not favoritism. That's wisdom.

Even Jesus had circles. If Jesus had circles, you're allowed to have circles too.

A word about different friendship wiring

Some people are 'one or two close friends' people.

Some people are 'lots of friends' people.

Some people recharge with people. Some people recharge alone.

None of those are moral issues. They're design differences.

The goal isn't to force yourself into someone else's friendship style.

The goal is to build a friendship life that reflects love, truth, and health.

If you're more introverted, you may need fewer friendships but deeper ones.

If you're more extroverted, you may enjoy a wider circle and more frequent connection.

Both can honor God. Both can be wise.

When friendship needs boundaries

Let's tell the truth: not every friendship is safe.

Some friendships are draining because they are one-sided.

Some friendships are draining because they are built on gossip or crisis.

Some friendships are draining because they require you to shrink to be included.

Boundaries aren't just for romantic relationships or workplaces. Boundaries are friendship kindness too.

Paul says, "Bad company corrupts good character" (1 Corinthians 15:33, NIV).

That verse isn't about becoming judgmental. It's about becoming wise.

Your friendships shape you. Your circle is a formation environment.

So if you're trying to build a healthy "us," be honest about what your friendships are producing in you.

A simple friendship audit (without shame)

Ask yourself three gentle questions:

- After time with this person, do I feel more alive or more depleted?
- Does this friendship call me toward the best of me—or toward the shadow of me?
- Is there mutual respect and mutual effort—or am I carrying the whole thing?

None of those questions are meant to produce guilt.

They're meant to produce clarity. Clarity is mercy.

Try this sentence

To build friendship with intention: "I value you, and I'd love to be more intentional about staying connected—what would that look like for you?"

To set a boundary without drama: "I care about you, and I'm not able to carry that the way I have been. Here's what I can do."

Optional reflection

1) Which circle do you need more of right now—fun, safe, or growth?

2) Who is already in your circle that you're grateful for? (Say their name. Gratitude matters.)

3) Is there one friendship boundary you need so your heart stays healthy?

Prayer

Father, thank You for the gift of friendship. Give me wisdom to build healthy circles—fun, safe, and growth-producing. Help me be a friend who loves well: present, honest, and kind. Teach me to set boundaries without bitterness and to invest where there is mutual honor. In Jesus' name, amen.

Bridge to Chapter 15

Friendships shape our personal world. Next, we're going to step into another environment where "us" matters every day: the workplace. In Chapter 15, we'll talk about building culture—ending 'us vs. them' and turning differences into supply.

Chapter 15: Workplace Culture — Ending 'Us vs. Them' and Building Team Supply

The workplace is one of the biggest community classrooms most of us will ever attend.

You don't get to pick every personality. You don't get to hand-select everyone's communication style.

And you don't get to say, "I'm just going to avoid humans for the next quarter."

So if you want to practice the 'us,' work will give you opportunities. Daily.

A healthy workplace isn't one where nobody disagrees.

A healthy workplace is one where people can disagree, problem-solve, and move forward without shaming, blaming, or dividing into camps.

Culture beats chemistry

Chemistry is "we click." Culture is "we can work well even when we don't click."

A business can have amazing chemistry on a good day and still collapse under pressure if there is no shared culture.

But a team with healthy culture can handle stress, change, and difference with maturity.

Culture is simply the repeated way people behave.

How we talk. How we decide. How we solve problems. How we handle tension. How we repair.

And culture always gets formed—either on purpose or by default.

The 'us vs. them' trap

One of the fastest ways a workplace turns toxic is when differences become personal.

Sales starts seeing operations as negative.

Operations starts seeing sales as careless.

Leadership starts seeing employees as resistant.

Employees start seeing leadership as out of touch.

And then the environment becomes more about protecting ego than serving mission.

This is where Book 2 language matters: difference isn't danger. Difference is often supply.

God designed people with different strengths because the work needs more than one lens.

A biblical picture of team design

Paul uses the body as a picture: "The body is not made up of one part but of many" (1 Corinthians 12:14, NIV).

Different parts, one purpose.

And he says something that feels very workplace-relevant: the parts that seem weaker are "indispensable" (1 Corinthians 12:22, NIV).

In other words: the person you don't naturally understand may be the person carrying a crucial piece of the mission.

The Workplace Main Thing

Remember Chapter 3: shared values, shared purpose, shared respect.

That is the main thing at work too.

Shared purpose: why we exist, who we serve, what we are building.

Shared values: how we behave while we build it.

Shared respect: the atmosphere that keeps people safe enough to contribute.

When the main thing is clear, people can disagree on methods and still stay aligned.

When the main thing is unclear, method differences become identity wars.

Five practices that clean up workplace culture

Here are five practices that change workplace culture without making it weird or overly "soft."

1) Honor language

Honor at work is simple: dignity in tone.

No sarcasm as leadership. No contempt as comedy.

Ephesians says our words should build (Ephesians 4:29, NIV). That applies at home and at work.

If your words make people smaller, your culture will shrink.

2) Translate instead of accuse

Instead of "They don't care," try "They may be protecting something."

Instead of "They're negative," try "They might be seeing risk we're missing."

Translation turns conflict into collaboration.

3) Shared rhythms

A lot of workplace stress is simply unclear rhythm: unclear meetings, unclear handoffs, unclear expectations.

A weekly **rhythm**—what we're building, what's blocked, who owns what—reduces conflict drastically (Chapter 6).

4) Decision clarity

Most workplace drama is unclear decision rights.

Decide / Advise / Inform is not complicated, but it is powerful (Chapter 7).

5) Quick repair

Teams that repair quickly don't stay stuck in tension.

A leader who can say, "That came out wrong—let me try again," builds trust faster than the leader who is always right but never humble (Chapter 9).

A practical scenario: big-picture vs detail-first

Imagine a team working on a project.

The big-picture person wants momentum. The detail-first person wants accuracy.

Both are gifts.

Without honor, they become enemies.

With honor, they become supply.

A leader can say: "We need both lenses. For this stage, we prioritize speed. For the next stage, we prioritize precision. Let's define what 'good enough' means right now."

That sentence alone can prevent weeks of friction.

Workplace boundaries that bless

Work also requires boundaries—because over-functioning creates resentment, and resentment creates toxicity.

Colossians says, "Whatever you do, work at it with all your heart, as working for the Lord" (Colossians 3:23, NIV).

Working with your whole heart doesn't mean working with no limits.

It means working with integrity.

Integrity includes honoring your capacity, your family, and your health—so your work remains life-giving.

Try this sentence

For leaders: "I want our culture to feel respectful and clear. Can we name what success looks like—and who owns what—so we can move forward together?"

For teammates: “I may be seeing this through a different lens. Can I show you what I’m noticing—so we don’t miss something important?”

For repair after tension: “That came out sharp. I’m for you. Can we reset and solve the problem?”

Optional reflection

1) Where does ‘us vs. them’ show up most in your workplace (between departments, between leaders and staff, between personalities)?

2) What is one practice that would shift the culture quickly (honor language, translation, rhythm, decision clarity, repair)?

3) What is one sentence you could use this week to build culture instead of blaming people?

Prayer

Father, thank You for meaningful work and the people we do it with. Give me wisdom to be a builder of healthy culture—honor, clarity, and peace. Help me see people as Your workmanship and treat them with dignity. Teach me to translate differences into supply and to repair quickly when we miss it. In Jesus' name, amen.

Bridge to Chapter 16

Culture needs leadership—at home, at work, and in community. In Chapter 16, we'll talk about leadership that serves: the difference between control and covering, and how to steward people with honor.

Chapter 16: Leadership that Serves — The Difference Between Control and Covering

Leadership is not a title. Leadership is influence.

And influence shows up everywhere—marriage, parenting, friendships, teams, communities, and yes, churches too.

But this book is not about institutional leadership. It's about how to steward people well—wherever God has placed you.

Healthy leadership doesn't try to make people smaller so the leader can feel bigger.

Healthy leadership creates safety, clarity, and growth.

I like to call it covering: not control, covering.

Control vs. covering

Control sounds like: "Do it my way." "Don't question me." "I'll decide; you comply."

Covering sounds like: "I'll protect what's healthy." "I'll clarify direction." "I'll make room for you to contribute."

Control is rooted in fear. Covering is rooted in stewardship.

Jesus gave us the clearest leadership definition in one sentence: "Whoever wants to become great among you must be your servant" (Matthew 20:26, NIV).

Servant leadership doesn't mean you avoid decisions. It means your decisions are for the good of others, not the inflation of your ego.

A biblical picture: Nehemiah builds culture

Nehemiah didn't just rebuild a wall. He rebuilt morale.

He organized people by families and roles. He created shared purpose. He addressed fear. He dealt with opposition.

And he kept calling people back to the main thing: "The joy of the Lord is your strength" (Nehemiah 8:10, NIV).

That's leadership: strengthening people so they can build together.

Healthy leaders do three things well:

- They clarify purpose (why we're here).
- They protect people (how we treat each other).
- They create pathways (how we move forward).

Leadership begins with self-leadership

Before you can lead others well, you have to lead yourself. Self-leadership looks like: regulating your tone, owning your mistakes, and refusing to let your shadow run the room. It's saying, "I'm going to respond with wisdom, not reaction."

Proverbs says, "Better a patient person than a warrior, one with self-control than one who takes a city" (Proverbs 16:32, NIV).

That verse is leadership gold. Self-control is a form of strength. And leaders who can regulate become safe leaders.

The culture questions every leader should ask

Whether you lead a team of two or a family of six, these questions build culture fast:

- What do we want to be true about us when we're under pressure?
- What behaviors will we protect—and what behaviors will we address quickly?
- How do we handle conflict here?
- How do we repair here?
- How do we make room for different lenses without shaming them?

If you can answer those questions clearly, you will build an environment where people can contribute without walking on eggshells.

Power is a trust

Leadership always involves some form of power—decision power, influence power, access power.

And power is a trust.

It's not a license to demand. It's a responsibility to serve.

Jesus said, "From everyone who has been given much, much will be demanded" (Luke 12:48, NIV).

That includes the power to influence people.

How to lead difference without favoritism

Leaders often have a natural tendency to favor people who are like them.

They feel easier. They communicate the same way. They validate the leader's style.

But if you only empower mirrors, you'll create a narrow culture—and you'll miss vital supply.

Covering leadership makes room for different designs.

It doesn't treat difference as defiance.

It asks: "What does this person bring that we need?"

And then it provides the clarity and support that helps that gift flourish.

Try this sentence

"I don't need you to be like me to contribute here. I do need us to share values, purpose, and respect. Let's name what that looks like."

And for leaders after a hard moment:

"That came out too sharp. I own that. Here's what I was trying to protect, and here's what I want to build with you."

Optional reflection

1) Where do you have influence right now (home, work, friendships, community)?

2) When you feel stressed, do you drift toward control or covering? What are you trying to protect?

3) What is one culture question you could ask this week that would strengthen your 'us'?

Prayer

Father, make me a leader who serves. Teach me to cover people with honor and clarity, not control. Give me wisdom to build culture that reflects You—truthful, kind, and strong. Help me steward influence with humility and courage. In Jesus' name, amen.

Bridge to Chapter 17

Leadership sets culture, but the goal of this book is not just ideas—it's a blueprint. In Chapter 17, we'll put everything together into a simple 'How we do us here' template you can use at home, work, or anywhere God has placed you.

Chapter 17: The Community Blueprint — "How We Do Us Here" (A Simple Template)

If you've made it this far, you already know something powerful: healthy community isn't magic. It's built.

And it's built with repeated practices—honor, translation, shared rhythms, decision clarity, clean conflict, quick repair, boundaries, and belonging.

Now we're going to put it all together in one simple blueprint you can use anywhere: home, work, friendship circles, teams, and community groups.

This is not meant to feel heavy. It's meant to feel doable.

You're not writing a constitution. You're building a culture.

And culture changes with one clear conversation at a time.

The Blueprint in one page

Here is the template. You can use all of it or start with one section.

1) Our Main Thing

Values: What do we protect here?

Purpose: Why are we together—what are we building?

Respect: How do we treat each other, especially under pressure?

2) Our Rhythms

Connection: How do we stay close?

Communication: How do we talk about hard things?

Planning: How do we handle schedules, responsibilities, and expectations?

Repair: How do we reset when we miss it?

3) Our Decisions

Who decides what? Who needs to be consulted?

Who just needs to be informed?

4) Our Conflict

What do we do when we get heated?

What language is off-limits (sarcasm, contempt, threats, silent punishment)?

What does 'truth without heat' look like for us?

5) Our Boundaries

What behaviors will we address quickly? What will we do if respect breaks down? What limits protect peace and keep love sustainable?

6) Our Belonging

How do we make room for different designs and different lenses?

How do we include people without losing ourselves?

How do we celebrate contribution—especially quiet contribution?

A simple way to start (without a long meeting)

If the word blueprint makes you want to run, I get it.

So here's a simple way to start in under fifteen minutes:

- Choose one value you want to protect (kindness, honesty, steadiness, generosity).
- Choose one rhythm you want to build (weekly check-in, calendar review, quick repair phrase).
- Choose one sentence you will use when things get tense ("I'm for you. Can we reset?").

Start there. Small changes practiced consistently become culture.

A note for different wiring

If you're a list person, you'll love a written blueprint.

If you're a spontaneous person, you may love having just a few anchor phrases.

Both are valid.

The goal is not to do it perfectly. The goal is to do it intentionally.

God can work with intentional.

Try this sentence

"Can we name one value, one rhythm, and one repair phrase we want to practice—so our 'us' gets stronger over time?"

Optional reflection

1) If you could protect one value in your relationships right now, what would it be?

2) What is one rhythm that would bring peace quickly?

3) What sentence would help you stay in honor when stress rises?

Prayer

Father, thank You for creating us for connection. Give me wisdom to build culture on purpose—values, purpose, and respect. Teach me to practice honor, translate differences with curiosity, and repair quickly. Help my life become a place where people can breathe and grow. In Jesus' name, amen.

Bridge to Chapter 18

A blueprint gives direction—but sometimes wisdom requires adjustment. In Chapter 18, we'll talk about fit, fruit, and when it's wise to change patterns, change environments, or even separate paths without bitterness.

Chapter 18: When to Adjust, When to Separate — Fit, Fruit, and Wisdom

One of the most mature things you can learn in relationships is this: not every environment is a good fit for your design.

And not every connection can be close—at least not in the same way—if there isn't shared respect.

This book is about building "us."

But building "us" doesn't mean forcing "us" where wisdom says it isn't healthy.

Sometimes the most loving thing you can do is adjust the pattern.

Sometimes the most loving thing you can do is adjust the environment.

And sometimes the most loving thing you can do is separate paths—with clean hands and a soft heart.

Wisdom is not the same as rejection

Many of us carry a fear that if we step back, we are failing.

But stepping back can be wisdom.

Even Jesus sometimes withdrew. He moved on from places that demanded a spectacle. He didn't force closeness where hearts were closed.

That wasn't rejection. That was alignment.

Scripture shows us moments of separation too.

Paul and Barnabas—two strong leaders who loved Jesus—had such a sharp disagreement that they separated (Acts 15:36–41, NIV).

That story doesn't celebrate division. It shows reality: sometimes two good people cannot move forward together in the same assignment.

And yet God still used both of them.

There is a difference between separation in bitterness and separation in wisdom.

Bitterness punishes. Wisdom protects.

Bitterness gossips. Wisdom stays clean.

Bitterness rehearses the offense. Wisdom learns the lesson.

Three wisdom filters: Fit, Fruit, and Freedom

When you're trying to discern whether to adjust or separate, these three filters can help:

1) Fit

Fit asks: Is this environment compatible with who God designed me to be?

This isn't about comfort. It's about alignment.

If your wiring requires creativity and your environment demands rigid control, you may constantly feel like you are failing—even if you're not.

If your wiring requires structure and your environment demands constant improvisation, you may feel anxious and depleted—even if you're capable.

Fit doesn't mean the environment has to match you perfectly.

But it does mean the environment can't require you to betray your God-given design to survive.

2) Fruit

Fruit asks: What is this producing in me over time?

Not one bad day. Over time.

Is it producing love, joy, peace, patience—even through challenge?

Or is it producing anxiety, dread, resentment, and a constant shadow self?

Jesus said we would recognize trees by their fruit (see Matthew 7:16, NIV).

That principle is helpful here.

Sometimes the loudest wisdom is simply noticing what's being produced in your soul.

3) Freedom

Freedom asks: Do I have room to obey God here?

Not just room to perform—but room to obey.

Does this environment allow you to live with integrity? To speak truth? To set boundaries? To grow?

Or does it demand fear-based compliance?

Paul says, "It is for freedom that Christ has set us free" (Galatians 5:1, NIV).

Freedom doesn't mean you do whatever you want.

It means you are not ruled by fear, manipulation, or bondage.

Adjust first (when possible)

Before you separate, wisdom often says: adjust what you can adjust.

Sometimes a relationship improves dramatically with one honest conversation.

Sometimes a team improves with clearer roles.

Sometimes a marriage improves with new rhythms and quick repair.

Sometimes a family improves when parents unite around values and respect.

Sometimes a friendship improves when boundaries become clean.

In other words: don't jump to separation when you haven't tried clarity.

Clarity is kindness.

But don't stay where respect is absent

We also need to say this clearly: if there is no mutual respect—if someone consistently dishonors you, manipulates you, shames you, or harms you—wisdom may require distance.

This book has intentionally used Scripture stories to talk about toxicity without turning the whole book into a trauma manual.

But we will not pretend disrespect is love.

If there is no shared main thing—no shared respect, no shared willingness to honor—then you cannot build healthy "us" no matter how hard you try.

And wise people let that information guide their next steps.

How to separate with clean hands

If you need to step back, here are four principles that keep your heart healthy:

- Stay truthful: don't rewrite history, but don't exaggerate it either.
- Stay honoring: you can disagree without demonizing.
- Stay bounded: protect your peace with clear limits.
- Stay open to God: let Him lead the next season.

Sometimes separation is permanent. Sometimes it's a season.

Sometimes it's relational distance but still basic kindness.

Sometimes it's changing roles while keeping love.

Wisdom is not one-size-fits-all.

Try this sentence

"I'm committed to staying honoring. And for my health, I need to step back from this pattern. If things change, we can revisit. For now, I'm choosing distance with respect."

And if you're adjusting rather than separating:

"I want to stay connected, and I need us to change the pattern. Can we name what we're protecting and build a new rhythm?"

Optional reflection

1) Where are you forcing closeness that doesn't have shared respect?

2) Use the filters: what do you notice about fit, fruit, and freedom in this relationship or environment?

3) What is one adjustment you can try before you consider stepping back?

Prayer

Father, give me wisdom. Teach me when to persevere, when to adjust, and when to step back. Keep my heart free from bitterness and my hands clean. Help me honor others without abandoning myself. Lead me into environments where I can bear good fruit and walk in freedom. In Jesus' name, amen.

Bridge to Chapter 19

This book has been about building "us" with wisdom. Now we're going to lift our eyes and see the bigger picture: what kind of community reflects heaven on earth. In Chapter 19, we'll talk about joyful witness—how a healthy 'us' becomes light to the world.

Chapter 19: A Community That Looks Like Heaven — Joyful Witness in Real Life

When God builds a healthy "us," it doesn't just bless the people inside it. It becomes light to the people around it.

In a world that is tired of division, tired of outrage, and tired of performative kindness, a community marked by honor stands out.

Not because it's perfect. Because it's real.

Jesus said, "By this everyone will know that you are my disciples, if you love one another" (John 13:35, NIV).

Notice what He didn't say.

He didn't say the world would know by our arguments, our volume, our labels, or our ability to win debates.

He said love would be the marker.

And love is not vague. Love has shape. Love has practices.

Heaven culture starts now

Sometimes people think heaven is only a future hope.

But Scripture also teaches that God's kingdom is breaking in now.

We get to live like citizens of that kingdom in real time.

That means our homes, friendships, and workplaces can become small outposts of heaven culture:

- honor instead of contempt
- truth instead of performance
- repair instead of bitterness
- clarity instead of chaos
- belonging instead of exclusion

This is not naïve optimism. This is intentional discipleship.

It's choosing the way of Jesus in daily life.

What makes a community feel like heaven?

A community that looks like heaven is not one where everyone is the same.

It's one where difference is held in love.

It's one where people can disagree without degrading.

It's one where weak moments are met with help, not humiliation.

It's one where the quiet contributor is honored.

It's one where leaders serve and people grow.

Paul paints this picture beautifully: "Clothe yourselves with compassion, kindness, humility, gentleness and patience. Bear with each other and forgive one another… And over all these virtues put on love" (Colossians 3:12–14, NIV).

That's heaven culture clothing.

And it's available now.

The 'us' is your witness

You don't have to stand on a street corner with a microphone to be a witness.

A healthy 'us' is a witness.

When your marriage has honor, people notice.

When your parenting has peace, people notice.

When your workplace culture is respectful, people notice.

When your friendships are safe and growth-producing, people notice.

And because God has stamped His image into the human heart, people are already hungry for love that is real.

When they taste it—even a little—it becomes contagious.

Keep the main thing the main thing

As you build community, don't get lost in secondary things.

Unity is not always agreement.

The main thing is values, purpose, and respect.

The practices are honor, translation, rhythm, clarity, clean conflict, repair, boundaries, and belonging.

And the power behind it all is the presence of God—alive in you.

This is not self-help. This is Spirit-empowered transformation.

You are not building alone.

God is with you. God is in you.

And He is still delighting in His people—very good workmanship, learning how to live together.

Try this sentence

"What would it look like for our home / team / circle to feel like an outpost of heaven—more honor, more peace, more truth, more love?"

Optional reflection

1) Where has God been strengthening your 'us' as you've read this book?

2) What practice changed the atmosphere most for you (honor, translation, rhythm, repair, boundaries, belonging)?

3) What is one place you want to become 'heaven culture' this month—your home, your friendships, your workplace?

Prayer

Father, thank You for building us into Your family and giving us Your Spirit. Make my life an outpost of heaven—full of love, truth, honor, and joy. Help me build community with wisdom and compassion. Teach me to keep the main thing the main thing, and to practice Your way in daily life. Let the love of Jesus be contagious through the 'us' You're building. In Jesus' name, amen.

Bridge to the Epilogue

You don't have to change everything overnight. You just have to keep building. In the Epilogue, we'll talk about small steps, steady practices, and how God uses faithful builders over time.

Epilogue: Keep Building — Small Steps, Steady Love

If you've read this far, I want you to hear this clearly: you're already doing the work.

The fact that you're thinking about honor, translation, rhythm, repair, boundaries, and belonging means you're moving from autopilot to intentional.

And intentional is where change begins.

Most of us want community to feel better overnight.

But God usually builds strong things the same way He grows strong people—slowly, faithfully, and with daily choices.

That's not discouraging. That's hopeful.

Because it means you don't have to fix everything at once.

You just have to keep building.

The 'us' grows by practice, not perfection

A healthy "us" isn't built by finding the perfect people.

It's built by practicing the right things with the people you already have:

- honor language when stress rises
- curiosity before conclusions
- clear roles and rhythms so life is workable
- truth without heat
- quick repair when you miss it
- boundaries that protect peace
- belonging that makes room for design

None of that requires a spotlight. It requires faithfulness.

And faithfulness is one of the quietest forms of spiritual power.

A simple 30-day build (if you want it)

If you want a simple rhythm to help you apply this book without turning your life into homework, try this 30-day build:

- Week 1: Practice honor. Use one honor sentence every day.
- Week 2: Practice translation. Ask one curiosity question before you assume.
- Week 3: Practice repair. Don't let distance sit—reset quickly.

- Week 4: Practice boundaries and belonging. Set one clean boundary and widen the circle once.

That's it. Four weeks. Small steps. Real change.

When you fail (because you will sometimes)

You will have moments where you say it wrong.

You will have moments where you react instead of respond.

You will have days where your shadow shows up before your wisdom does.

That doesn't mean you're not growing. It means you're human.

The win is not "I never mess up." The win is "I repair quickly and keep building."

Scripture says, "His mercies never come to an end; they are new every morning" (Lamentations 3:22–23, NLT).

New mercies mean you can begin again—with God and with people.

Remember what God is doing

God is not just trying to make you nice.

He is forming Christ in you. And Christ in you changes the way you build relationships.

As you live intentionally connected to the God who created you, you become more like who you were designed to be—and you become more able to recognize and honor who others were designed to be too.

That's how communities change.

Not by perfection. By people who keep choosing love on purpose.

Try this sentence

"I don't want to be right; I want us to be healthy. Can we take one small step toward each other today?"

Optional reflection

1) What practice from this book changed your atmosphere the most?

2) What is one small habit you want to carry forward for the next 30 days?

3) Who is one person you want to build 'us' with on purpose? What is one sentence you can use to start?

Prayer

Father, thank You for building us into Your family and for teaching us how to love. Help me keep building with steady courage—honor, truth, kindness, and strength. When I miss it, make me quick to repent and quick to repair. Let the 'us' You build in my life reflect Your heart to the world. In Jesus' name, amen.

Appendix A: The Community Blueprint

If you want to print something, screenshot something, or put something on the fridge (or in the team folder), this is it.

You can use this in a marriage, a family, a friendship circle, a workplace team, or any community you're building.

1) Our Main Thing

Values: What do we protect here?

Purpose: Why are we together—what are we building?

Respect: How do we treat each other, especially under pressure?

2) Our Rhythms

Connection: How do we stay close?

Communication: How do we talk about hard things?

Planning: How do we handle schedules, responsibilities, and expectations?

Repair: How do we reset when we miss it?

3) Our Decisions

Who decides what?

Who needs to be consulted?

Who needs to be informed?

4) Our Conflict

What do we do when we get heated?

What language is off-limits (sarcasm, contempt, threats, silent punishment)?

What does 'truth without heat' look like for us?

5) Our Boundaries

What behaviors will we address quickly?

What will we do if respect breaks down?

What limits protect peace and keep love sustainable?

6) Our Belonging

How do we make room for different designs and different lenses?

How do we include people without losing ourselves?

How do we celebrate contribution—especially quiet contribution?

Appendix B:
"Try This Sentence" Quick List

Use these like tools, not scripts. You're not trying to sound perfect—you're trying to stay in honor.

Pick one. Try it once. Repair quickly if you say it wrong. That counts as growth.

Honor

- "You matter to me. Can we talk about this with honor?"
- "I'm for you. I'm not against you. I just want us to be healthy."

Unity without agreement

- "We don't have to agree on everything to stay in honor. Can we stay connected while we sort this out?"
- "Help me understand what matters most to you about this."

Translation

- "Before I assume, help me understand how you got there."
- "What are you trying to protect right now?"

Rhythms

- "Can we build a simple rhythm for this so we stop re-fighting the same problem?"
- "I don't need a perfect plan—I just need a predictable moment of you."

Decisions

- "Who is the decider, who needs to be consulted, and who just needs to be informed?"
- "I can say yes to this if we can also say no to that."

Conflict

- "I'm not trying to win—I'm trying to understand and build something healthy."
- "I want to talk about this, but I'm not in a good tone right now. Can we pause and come back?"

Repair

- "That didn't come out the way I meant. Can I try again—with cleaner words?"
- "I'm sorry. I own that. I'm for you."

Boundaries

- "I can do this, but not that."
- "If we can't speak with respect right now, I'm going to step back and we can revisit this later."

Belonging

- "I'm glad you're here. Your perspective matters."
- "You don't have to be like me to belong with me."

About the Author

Cindy H. Carr began her faith journey on December 24, 1984. It didn't begin in a church service or with an altar call, but through a personal invitation from Jesus Christ while she was alone preparing for Christmas Eve. In that quiet moment, a relationship was born—one that transcended theology, tradition, and every expectation of what faith was "supposed" to be.

Over the decades that followed, Cindy immersed herself in theological study and served in both business and her community, yet her unwavering relationship with Jesus Christ has guided every step of her life and leadership. She has learned that love—steady, simple, and sincere—is the foundation strong enough to endure any storm.

In *God Made Us, And He Does Not Make Junk*, Cindy concludes the trilogy by bringing identity and difference into shared life—family, friendship, work teams, and community. With Scripture and real-world application, Cindy helps readers learn how to create environments where uniquely designed people can belong and thrive.

www.ingramcontent.com/pod-product-compliance
Lightning Source LLC
LaVergne TN
LVHW010949110826
845149LV00015B/3277

9781971192055